Being Brave

Soumini Menon

BookLeaf Publishing

India | USA | UK

Presentation by *BookLeaf Publishing*

Web: www.bookleafpub.com

E-mail: info@bookleafpub.com

ISBN: 9789363319950

First edition 2024

To Nikhil who taught me how to love.

*To Imaara and Azaan who taught me how
to thrive.*

ACKNOWLEDGEMENT

Thank you, to all the people and places that keep the dance in me alive.

Why Do I Care?

I don't know your story but I see your pain
And your pain stirs in me a feeling unknown to
me
Your story reminds me of many of mine and
when the time is right I will share
But not today, not now

I don't know why or how or the answer to your
problem
Coz you are not the problem
It is this feeling
So, till you get ready
I will wait for you by your side
To seek the light in the darkness
To seek the rainbow after the rain

I am here, yes, and I am ready, to listen
I am here, yes, and I am ready, I see you
I am here, yes, and I am ready, to hold your hand
I am here, yes, and I am ready, to stay with you

My Tribe

If we are ever so lucky
Every once in a while
We chance upon people beyond our family
That becomes part of our history

If we look out, each one of us will find
We have been blessed to have met many along
the way.
Some have been there for a brief moment
But have shaped us to be who we are today

But there are a few, who become your tribe,
Who are there for life
They have seen you at your worst
And have celebrated you at your best.

They can call you out when you are lying to
yourself
And yet protect you like a strong shield from
others' wrath.

And each one of us needs that tribe
That 'sees us', for us unconditionally.
And that defines our soul sisters (or our
brothers).

So, recognise it, embrace it, and fiercely protect
this tribe
Because we are not perfect
But, so what?
Our friendships definitely can be

Parenting with Courage

Everyone says and now I do believe
That there is no bigger gift than the birth of a
child
But no one says and now I do know
That it's a whole new way of life with no
guidelines

And now I shall share today for all to know
Despite all the joy, it's a road for the brave
Because it takes courage to give birth,
But it takes greater courage to be reborn as a
parent

It takes courage to hold a tiny life in your arms
And to take them home without knowing the
path
It takes courage despite all these fears and
doubts
To feel unconditional love so strong, so loud.

It takes courage to let go of those skinny jeans
and crop tops
And embrace your stretch marks and shapeless
form

It takes courage to hold your baby through the
night
While you try to console a weeping wife by your
side

It takes courage to sit down and not take a quick
nap
While your child looks happy and engrossed in
play
It takes courage despite all the aches, bruises,
and weight
To go out and carry your child all the way

It takes courage to stay calm and quiet
When you spend sleepless nights full of cries
It takes courage to persist in feeding and not
walk out
Even when there may be no triumphs despite so
many hours

It takes courage to spend stressful days writing
essays
To make sure your child gets the best school in
the state
And then it takes more courage to let go of their
little hands
As they walk into a whole new land through
those gates

It takes courage to fight the urge to cry
When they have their first fall or fight
And it takes courage after crazy schedules and
exhausted days
To watch them with their grandparents all happy
and gay

It takes courage to say, 'No' to them
As tears roll down their cheeks
It takes courage to not run away
When they lie down on the floor and scream

It takes courage to stay in your room
When they say they need space
It takes courage to be fine
When all you need is more time

It takes courage to forgive yourself
When you know there are no do-overs
When you don't have the answers
And try to move forward

It takes courage to put your feet up
And to say not today not now
It takes courage to say that,
"Today, I come first"
I need some time to be mine

It takes courage to reinvent the parenting wheel
When your family doesn't fit the typical bill
It takes courage to watch your child fight their
battles
When all you can do is cheer from the sidelines

It takes the courage to ask for help
When despite being the parent you don't have
the answers
It takes the courage to tell your story to the
world
Even if you are not perfect, know it's your best

But it doesn't take courage to love them
To hug them
To laugh with them
And to cry with them
To be, just be with them

Because there is no doubt that parenting is a
road for the brave
But isn't it all worth it, for that sweet smile and
loving gaze
And it's scary, loud, and full of doubts
But if you ask me, I will never go back even
now.

My Darlings

Let me hold you a little more before you run
away...
Let me take you everywhere with me before you
want to go alone...
Let me take care of you until you have to take
care of yours...
Let me love you a little more before you are not
little anymore.

Sleepless Nights

I lie in bed
Staring at the shadows
I turn to my side and
I see you by my side
I wonder why I fear
When you are here
But a happy heart
Can't quiet the restless mind

I walk down the corridors
Staring at the photos on the wall
Places, faces, and smiles
What a good life it is
But a happy heart
Can't quiet the restless mind

I stare at the moon
And all that shines in its light
Hoping to calm the shivers
I sway like the gentle breeze
But a happy heart
Can't quiet the restless mind

I tip-toed into the room
Back into bed
Kisses for the little one
And the happy heart smiles
And then you shift to the other side
And hug me tight
And the big bear arms
Quiets down the restless mind

My Waye

Have I told you lately?
How much I love you?
Maybe last night
But I feel it again
This love, so loud
This love, so strong
This love for you
I can feel it all the time

I felt it the first time
When we sat under the moonlight
Laughing over my silly jokes
And it all felt so right
I felt it again
When we watched movies together
Not knowing then
This was going to be us, forever

I felt it again
When the music comes on
And you would sway me on the dance floor
Like the lyrics were written for you and I

I felt it again
When you said, *"I love you"*,
For the first time

Something you'd been holding in for a while

I felt it again for sure
When you asked my parents for my hand
And proposed in front of everyone we love
Under that beautiful starlit sky

I felt it again, when
We had our moments of loss and heartbreak
But we stood strong by each other's side
Unwavering, holding each other's hands tight

I felt it again
When I walked down the aisle
With no doubt in my mind
To take the vows, to be your wife

I felt it again
When I cried in your arms
When we got to know we were growing
Unprepared, unknowing

I felt it again
When you cried, though you deny
When you held our little ones
For the very first time

I felt it again when we had our fights
And breakdowns and heartaches

And still held each other's hand
Refusing to let go
Choosing each other
Even when we were broke

I felt it again
When I would have my panic attacks
And you would sit peacefully next to me
Holding me tight and helping me breathe

The truth is my darling, *Waye*
I may have all the strength and *Will*
But at the end of the day, even
Will always need to find her Way(e)

Little Fights

How do you have those fights?
How do you put forward those thoughts
That hurt and sadden you
But are not reasons enough
To stop loving you

How do you prevent arguments?
About moments that break you
And the talk will not be easy
Coz we both have been hurt
And see it all in different lights

And they are a bit problematic
And not so traumatic
Coz we are not mean
But we are simply opposites
So, that moment can be exhausting

I know you can't change
And neither will I
But we will keep having these conversations
Again and again
Oh! So many times.

About how we can do things differently
And try to be better
Especially, for each other
But where will it take us
In a day, or two, or even a week

So, do we just choose not to speak?
And cry silently
About those little slips and misses
Or have those loud fights
Which will lead us to hate for a while

But not hate forever
Coz at the end of the day
They are the little things
And in this, you versus me versus us
The bigger picture is, that
You and I are meant to be

Chiki and Mini

Once upon a time
A timid little star lived
Unsure of herself
Twinkling dimly

One fine day
She met a bright ray of sunshine
Who shone through her
And cast all the colors of the rainbow

Where ever she went
The rays of the sun shined bright
Casting tall shadows on her
All over her fears

When it got dark
It would still be with her
Hiding behind the moon
Making her shine and glow

That ray of sunshine
Became her best friend
And in her company
She found her own sparkle

And though they were so small
Together, they grew
And their combined light
could not be dimmed

Together they shone, never alone
And their light never felt feeble
Full of love, courage, and compassion
Till they each became the sun of their own
universe

Patience

Patience is the best gift
That a parent can give a child

Patience, when the little legs
Climb all over your tired body

Patience, when the little hands
Tug and pull you when you aren't looking

Patience, when the little mouth
Keep asking the same questions

Patience, when the little heart
Asks for less work and more love

Patience is the best gift
That a child can give a parent

Pandemic World

Sitting by the window
The blue sky beckons me
I put my hand out
And the winds caress me
I take a deep breath
And the fresh air uplifts me

Oh! How you toy with my feelings
You tempt me to break the rules
And forget about today
To be 'one' again with you

And then in the distance
The TV blares
And it bursts my bubble
And, here I am

I got to stay in
There is no other way
This comfortable prison of mine
Will keep me safe
From plundering your abundance
And letting you waste

I thought I was the smart one
With a heart and a mind
With all the answers
On how to thrive

But you, my dear, mother
You were the only one
Who knew from the start
Who would be free
So, now at night when I lie in bed
I will forever cherish you in my dreams

One More Chance

Another day
A promise broken
But the wish stays
So, don't fret dear heart
Coz I shall try again
Tomorrow and the next day
In every possible way

No matter how much work
Or all the exhausting chores
My anger I shall hold
And keep love afloat
And when I am lost
And in my zone
I will let you creep in
And always hold

My space
My hand
My eyes
My heart

So, into the night
A promise I make
Even if the days feel hazy

My hugs won't get lazy
And at times we will cry
But we shall also smile
Most importantly
I shall try again
Tomorrow and the next day
In every possible way

Imaara

Dancing sunlight
Through the curtains
It's barely dawn
Exhausted I walk over
To start the drill
And there they are
Those bright shiny eyes
Full of wonder

The sky is dark
And the starry lights twinkle
No wake-up calls
Just bedtime stories
As I turn over
There they are
Those bright shiny eyes
Full of wonder

Years have passed
So much has changed
But something remains
Those loving reminders
My pick-me-up,
My energizer, my relaxant
Those bright shiny eyes
Full of wonder

Lead The Way

From the start of the lockdown
All I see is a wide grin on my screen
Behind closed doors
Actually, shut down laptops
What happens stays in your mind
And your actions and words rarely give a sign

But I have been watching
Though, it's you who has to see
I can't help but notice in you
All that's really unseen

You have so much heart
To take in all of us
Our work, our fears,
Our anger, our despair
You stand with open arms
To fill us with sweet dreams

You have so much courage
To never back away
To fight and find answers
And sometimes give space
But fiercely you stand
Like you are bulletproof
At the doors of our workspace

But, seems like at our hearts too

You have so much humor
For the best of celebrations
Or to lighten up the room
In the darkest of moments
Tempting us to stop fighting
And just accept it
That the jokes are here to stay
And will pop up from time to time

But more than ever
What I hadn't seen so far
The myriad of emotions
You so carefully guard
So vulnerable
So honest
So transparent
So real

Thank you, for showing me that side
And trusting me with it
It makes me feel confident
That I can be your ally
But mostly it has made you
An even greater leader
In my heart, my mind
And in my eyes

A New Friend

The other night
A friend came over
And we discussed our days
Of work and home
And casually I quipped
I miss my lazy morning coffee
And all she gave me
was an acknowledging smile

Days went by and I forgot that night
Till I heard knock on my door
Delivery for Soumini
From a caring friend

And here I am with my very own
coffee maker and all that jazz
But most importantly
My lazy morning coffee
Full of love and heart

And in that moment I realized
As an individual we are whole
But together, we are more

Virtual Friendships

Dear friend,
It's been a while
Since I saw your smile
And sparkling eyes

We hugged and laughed
Over coffee or wine
Teased each other
And sometimes sang in rhymes

But in these crazy times
The gifs and memes had to do
Insta challenges and bingos
Virtually anything to be with you

So, all I wanted to say was
Thanks for standing by
Always full of quips and cheer
Through all the lows and highs

The meetings might become less
But this tribe will not die
Through every tear and smile
I promise you
This sisterhood is for life

Goodbye

As a large beating heart
You stepped into my life
And like a wise old man
You guided my path
And before I knew it
I felt empowered
And ready to take on any challenge
That life had to offer

For the first time
The doubts subsided
I can do this
Is the chant that I hear
Ringing through my thoughts
And then there was no fear

Baby steps I took
Soon, I started to thrive
For the first time, I trusted my intuition
My hopes and desires
And when I became my own
And felt wholesome
Quietly, you said unsaid words
To unravel my threads

How do I take your power away?
To control my thoughts
To ripen my insecurities
To make me feel unsure
And that I have no vision
And there is a hidden intent

You gave me the confidence
To stand on my feet
But it seems the dance, now I choose
As per you, has a different beat

Does that scare you?
And make you feel weird
That, the one you mentored
Could also be a leader
And so you question my choices
And all of my actions
When all I think is
Please listen...

You and I are not different
We want the same
And maybe I can also do it
Give me a turn
Trust in me
Maybe, it might be different
But until you let go
How will I ever grow?

Nature

With all my heart, I surrender to you
To calm me with your gentle breeze
And the whispering willows to sing to me
While the floating clouds remind me to breathe
Under the twinkling stars and faint familiar laughter
I find a part of me, ready to be me again

Azaan

Every day you inspire me to fight my inner
demons
Every day you inspire me to ask difficult
questions
Every day you inspire me to make a difference
Every day you inspire me to live a life full of
courage

Memories

Days under blue skies
Foggy lenses and clear minds
Endless giggles and big-big snuggles
Matching colors and forced nibbles
Oh! My baby, how will I treasure
Every little memory in this lifetime, forever

My Girls

That can make any mother so proud
One, as beautiful as the midnight sky
The other is as bright as a sunflower
One with the quiet mischief to make your heart
beam
The other, full of spunk and grit to swell your
chest with pride
Now it's up to you to guess who is who.
It's not a riddle to be solved but an adventure to
be lived

Neuro-Wonderful

They say you can't connect, but I see you cry
when your mother, leaves.
They say you have no emotions, but I hear you
laugh when I spin you around.

They say you can't communicate, but I feel you
touch me for more bubbles.
They say you can't think, but I see you organize
and match your toys.

They say you can't concentrate, but I watch you
for hours with your clay.
They say you flap your hands, but I see you
calming yourself down when you don't
understand.

They say you hit and bite, but I know you are
asking for help.
They say you are lost, but like me, you are
searching for a place to belong.

They say you are rigid in your ways, but you are
trying to make this unpredictable world of ours
predictable.

They say you can't make friends, but you return
to me day after day.

Every day you trust me and every day I invest in
you
Because I am supposed to teach and train you

Make sense of your world, and help you keep
pace
But it is you who taught me how to embrace
The simple pleasures of life

The first eye contact, the first smile, the first,
'Hi!'
Tickles and peek-a-boo, kisses and high fives.

Jumping on the trampoline, running bare feet on
wet grass
Singing and dancing till you collapse

Colouring and painting with your feet and
hands.
Saying no to things we just can't stand

You are unique, so innocent and true
There's nothing you can hide through your
smiles and cries.

I hope you know that I am not trying to change
you
Just help you, be you,
In a way, we can join you.

Roar

A girl so quiet, a girl so kind
walked into my life.
But even then, I did not know
Why, she would always be on my side

Her soft eyes and gentle smile
were hiding a lie
Coz behind that beautiful creative mind
hid a crazy fierce lion.

And the beauty of this lion
She roared only once in a while
and believe me,
You never wanted to hear it twice.

To have this lion by your side
was a thing of pride
Because it's not very easily
She chose an ally.

So, 20 years ago
She chose me to be in her life.
And, little did I know then
This would give me wings to fly!

Hey Sister!

Hey sister, do you remember the day I was born?
Did you always feel so protective?

Hey sister, remember me hugging you tight
when I used to sleep?
Did you always find me cute?

Hey sister, do you remember me shadowing you
around?
Did you always find me annoying?

Hey sister, do you remember me telling on you?
Did I always make you angry?

Hey sister, do you remember me staying up all
night to hear of your adventures?
Did you always find me a good listener?

Hey sister, do you remember me hiding your
secrets?
Did you always know I would have your back?

Hey sister do you remember me dressing like
you?
Did you always take that as a compliment?

Hey sister, do you know I cried to sleep when
you left for Chennai?
Did you know, that was the beginning of us
growing up?

Hey sister, do you know you are still my first
person to go to?
Did you know that being your sister was the best
part of my childhood?

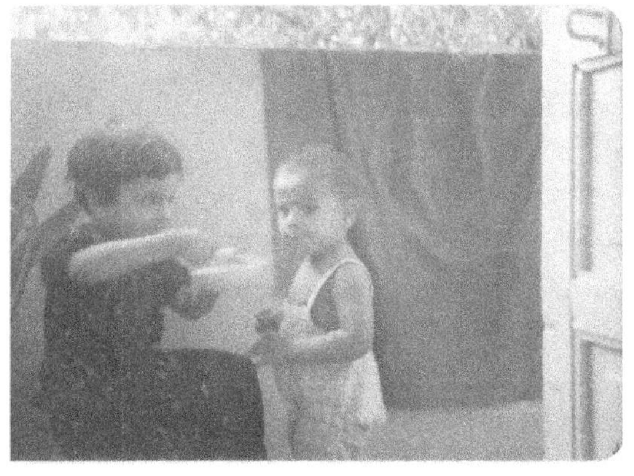

I See You

Today, I am just going to stay quiet
Because I have nothing more to say
Every word spoken has landed on a deaf ear
So, tonight I am not going to try

You say you want to help but you aren't even
open
To listen, to share my ideas and views
Or even if I care

So as I sit and watch you rant and tell your tales
again
I watch your face and suddenly I notice
Not the anger or rage but just the lines
Years of worries, years of wear and tear
All hidden behind this hard exterior of being
brave

When did your journey begin?
When did you first hurt?
When were you first turned away?
When did your heart break, first?
When did you face the harsh realities?
When did you first feel not good enough?

When did I first tell you, 'I hate you'?
When did you first grow up?

And yet, here you are in your best way, trying to
protect me
Helping me to be brave, to step out of my bubble
Maybe your way might not have been my way,
But all that matters is that you never gave up on
me.
You stood by me even when
It was hard, to just be.

Inside Stories

A broth brewed slowly
Churning quietly as it thickened
Not a single bubble or steam
No-one was aware

While it was on fire
Gaining its thickness
The little girl went about
Setting the table for a meal

She tried to match the dishes
For the meal to be served
For everyone, there was a piece
But hers was too big

So, she went about looking
And disappeared into the pantry
Looking for her favourite set
The one she had thought of will always be there

Suddenly the light went off
And she could see no more
What scared her more was that
She didn't know where to find the light

So, she lay down on the floor
And cried herself to sleep
Only to wake up to the aroma
Flowing in from the kitchen

She used her hands and feet
To find her way
To feel grounded, connected
With herself again

And as she pushed
She saw a beacon of light
Showing her a path
She waited no longer and followed it

The broth was still brewing
With little bubbles of flavour
Not a bland pale liquid
But now a myriad of colors

As she heard people arrive
She cleaned up and got ready
Today, she would be a big girl
With her big spoons and dish

But no one noticed
Or said a hurrah
Oh! it's what all girls do
Was the simple mantra

Oh, no! The brew has boiled over
Its spilled everywhere
What a mess for others to see
And what a mess to clear

As the girl mopped and cleared
She got scared and angry
What will everyone eat?
What more will she have to do?

As she got tired and slow
Ready to call it a night
She heard her stomach rumble
'I need a lot more'

So, like the woman she dreamt to be
She started the broth from scratch
She didn't know the recipe
Or how it should be

But from her memories and intuitions
She added most of the parts
From the books and manuals
She sprinkled her choices

And there, brew a beautiful broth
Full of life and color
Never seen or smelt before
That everyone collected on the kitchen floor

There was laughter and cheer
At the dinner table tonight
But the little girl sipped her broth, peacefully
Unaware of the noise

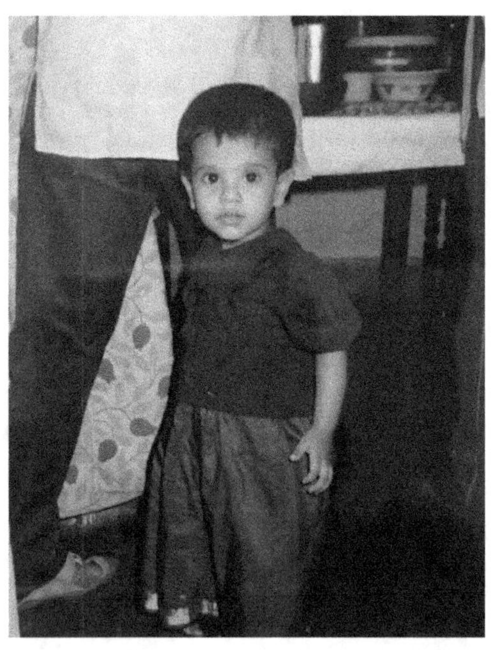